JOURNAL NOTEBOOK

DAILY JOURNAL NOTEBOOK FOR BOTH KIDS AND ADULTS| 6X9"

REYS NJOURNAL

To my best friend,

Always keep smiling and shining.

Contents

Dump All Your Thoughts Here. It's A Very Safe Place For You To Be Vulnerable.

1. Journal — 3
2. Journal — 4
3. Journal — 5
4. Journal — 6
5. Journal — 7
6. Journal — 8
7. Journal — 9
8. Journal — 10
9. Journal — 11
10. Journal — 12
11. Journal — 13
12. Journal — 14
13. Journal — 15
14. Journal — 16
15. Journal — 17
16. Journal — 18
17. Journal — 19
18. Journal — 20
19. Journal — 21
20. Journal — 22
21. Journal — 23
22. Journal — 24
23. Journal — 25
24. Journal — 26
25. Journal — 27
26. Journal — 28

Contents

27. Journal 29

28. Journal 30

29. Journal 31

30. Journal 32

Dump all your thoughts here. It's a very safe place for you to be vulnerable.

I

Journal

II
Journal

Date:

III

Journal

IV
Journal

Date:

V

Journal

Date:

VI

Journal

Date:

VII

Journal

Date:

VIII

Journal

Date:

IX

Journal

Date:

X

Journal

Date:

XI
Journal

Date:

XII

Journal

Date:

XIII

Journal

Date;

XIV

Journal

Date:

XV

Journal

Date:

XVI

Journal

Date:

XVII

Journal

Date:

XVIII

Journal

XIX
Journal

Date:

XX

Journal

Date:

XXI

Journal

Date:

XXII

Journal

Date:

XXIII

Journal

Date:

XXIV

Journal

Date:

XXV

Journal

Date:

XXVI

Journal

Date:

XXVII

Journal

Date:

XXVIII

Journal

Date:

XXIX

Journal

Date:

XXX

Journal

Date:

Thanks!